W9-BHG-002

Slumberkins®

This book belongs to

Scan here for additional Slumberkins resources and content.

Slumberkins®

Bigfoot Shares His Gift

By Kelly Oriard with Callie Christensen

Illustrated by Kristen Adam

One winter morning Bigfoot awoke
and jumped quickly out of bed.
"This is the day we all Shine Bright!
The festival is here!" he said.

This festival comes once a year,
when kins all celebrate
the love they have for everyone.
Bigfoot could hardly wait!

The kins bring special gifts
they make with love and care
that represent who they are
and spread joy everywhere.

1.

Bigfoot hummed a happy tune
    as he hurried down the stairs.
But his thoughts soon turned to worry,
    for he had no gift to share.

2.

Bigfoot plopped down next to his dad
his face filled with a frown.
"Today's the day of the festival!
What's got you feeling down?"

"Everyone else will have a gift
they made with love and care.
I tried to think of the perfect thing.
But I have nothing special to share."

3.

"I love that you want to give the kins
a special gift from you.
But you can do a gift with me
so you'll know just what to do.

Every year, I gather wood
to build the festival's fire.
I give the gift of warmth and light
for everyone to admire."

Bigfoot wanted his own gift to share,
    but the festival was so soon.
So he helped his dad gather wood,
    while he sang a little tune:

My dad is the best
    builder that I know!
He makes the biggest bonfire
    that helps Shine Bright to glow!

A rat ta ta da da
    a deet deet dee do do
a rat ta ta da dee da
    bee da ba da boo.

Yeah!

5.

Bigfoot's dad hugged his son
as they both walked along.

"You just made me so happy,
with your rockin' song."

6.

After the wood was gathered
   and stacked up nice and neat,
Bigfoot went out for a walk
   and followed a smell so sweet.

"Bigfoot!" called out Lynx and Yak,
   holding up their treats so proud—
each one rolled in sprinkles
   in shapes of trees and clouds.

7.

Yak gave Bigfoot a bite to taste:
   a cookie with sugar and spice.
He loved it so much he began to sing
   a melody so nice:

Cookies, cookies, sprinkle time,
   chewy in my face!
Yak and Lynx made such a treat
   to share with the whole place!

Dooba booba dooba dee
   ooba dooba dum—
When I eat these cookies,
   my mouth goes yummy yum!

8.

Yak and Lynx giggled with glee.
His song gave them such delight.
"Thanks for the kind compliment.
We can't wait to share them tonight!"

9.

Bigfoot said goodbye and thought
how lovely it would be
if he could bake a cake to share.
"But that's not uniquely me."

He kept on walking through the town
and saw more friends nearby.
Wolf and Ibex were making crafts;
the glitter caught his eye.

Bigfoot saw a stack of pinecones
covered in shiny gold
and tied together to make a crown—
a beautiful sight to behold.

He said hello and walked along,
　　with thoughts of twigs and twine.
"I could craft something to wear,
　　but that idea isn't mine."

He saw some familiar hoofprints
and followed them below.
He found Unicorn and Moose
building giant Kins from snow.

Unicorn tapped her hooves real quick.
   Glitter flew into the air
covering the Snowkins—
   just to add some flair.

Bigfoot had another song
and sung it for his friends.
They loved it so much they begged him
to sing it once again.

Moose can build a Snowkin
like none you've ever seen.
When Uni's glitter flies in the air,
the joy will make you scream!

Ahhhh ahhhh
glitter in the air!
Coming down to make us happy—
Glitter everywhere!

The sun was almost setting;
   there was no time left to roam.
"I'll see you tonight," Bigfoot said.
   And then he hurried home.

He walked right through the door,
   passing the lantern inside
that was shining dimly like
   his hopes. He sniffed; then cried:

17.

"I wish I had a gift to share,
with all my family and friends.
Something only I could give
before the festival ends."

18.

Bigfoot sighed and then recalled
    the kins he saw that day.
He'd brought them joy with a song
    in a unique Bigfoot way.

So he put them all together
    and sang with newfound cheer.
"Dad, I think I have a gift
    to help Shine Bright this year!"

"Yes, you do!" said Bigfoot's dad.
   "Gifts can be anything—
a treat to share of any size—
Your song is the perfect thing to bring."

Bigfoot's heart, so full of love,
   made the lantern glow more bright.
His gift had been there all along!
   Right there, just out of sight.

20.

The center of town was all lit up;
　　it twinkled like the stars.
The giant Snowkins were a hit,
　　just like Yak's cookie bars.

21.

The bonfire warmed up every kin,
crowned in gold and pine.
Bigfoot went up on the stage;
it was now his time to shine.

Bigfoot said, "I have a gift:
a **song** I want to share.
It's about the **special** ways
we show how much we care."

23.

The notes came out soft at first,
   until he felt **proud** and **strong**.
When the chorus came back again,
   every kin sang along:

I shine bright with others.
   I am as loved as can be.
A gift I can share
   is just being me!

I am loved just as I am;
   I can share my gift aloud.
I shine bright with others
   and I feel very proud!

Reflect & Connect

The holidays are a wonderful time to give and to share with others. In this book, the holiday season is brought to life through the magic of the Shine Bright Festival, where each kin shares a special gift with the community. This story reminds readers that showing up as your unique self is one of the greatest gifts of all.

Deepen the Learning

(1) How did Bigfoot feel at first when he didn't think he had a gift to share?

(2) What gift did Bigfoot realize he had to share? How did it make him feel? How did it make others feel?

(3) Do you have any holiday traditions that you celebrate in your family or community?

Adult Engagement: What gifts bring you joy to share with your community?

Slumberkins®

Discover a World of Feelings

From understanding emotions to strengthening their inner voice, give children the tools that support them to be caring, confident, and resilient.

The Caring Crew

IBEX — EMOTIONAL COURAGE | YETI — MINDFULNESS | SLOTH — ROUTINES | OTTER — BUILDING CONNECTIONS | HONEY BEAR — GRATITUDE

The Confidence Crew

BIGFOOT — SELF-ESTEEM | UNICORN — AUTHENTICITY | HAMMERHEAD — CONFLICT RESOLUTION | NARWHAL — GROWTH MINDSET | YAK — SELF-ACCEPTANCE

The Resilience Crew

FOX — CHANGE | ALPACA — STRESS RELIEF | SPRITE — GRIEF AND LOSS | LYNX — SELF-EXPRESSION | DRAGON — CREATIVITY